WHAT MUST I DO TO BE HEALED?

by
Billy B. Smith

All Scripture quotations are from the King James Version of the Bible unless otherwise indicated.

Scriptures from the New American Standard Bible are used by permission of The Lockman Foundation, La Habra, California © 1960-1977.

Printed in the United States of America.

Billy B. Smith Ministries Publications
P.O. Box 6078
Fort Worth, Texas 76115 U.S.A.

ISBN 1-879612-03-8

CONTENTS

I

REASONS FOR NOT BEING HEALED

The number one question I am asked about healing is, **"What must I do to be healed?"** The number two question I am asked is, **"Don't you believe it is God's will for some people to be sick?"** Both of these questions need to be answered, and with the help of the Holy Spirit I will answer them.

It has always amazed me how little people know about this subject that is so important to all of us. There is probably no one you know who has not experienced sickness and/or death, either personally or by some loved one.

Most people believe that sickness is just a part of life they can do nothing about. It is because of this attitude that many people live in sickness or become ill and die.

Hosea 4:6

My people are destroyed for lack of knowledge.

If you have never been taught that God wants to heal you, or that Jesus is the same yesterday, today, and forever, then you will never look for a change in your situation.

If you have not been taught that God is a healer and that He is healing today, then you will not go to Him for healing.

If you have been taught that God puts sickness on you to punish you or to teach you something, then you will not go to Him for healing. You may think He is still upset with you, and that He might put more sickness on you.

If you have been taught that God heals some people but does not want to heal others, the devil will always convince you that you are the one God does not want to heal.

Many people allow themselves to be trapped in their sick and crippled bodies because of someone else's experience or because of someone else's opinion. I want you to understand from the beginning of this book that my opinion and experience—or anyone else's—is not worth listening to if it does not agree with God's Word. We can only have faith to believe what comes from God's Word. The Bible gives only one way to build faith. Romans 10:17 says that faith comes from hearing God's Word—not from hearing someone's opinion or experience.

I have studied and preached God's Word for the last twenty-two years, and I have found only two scriptural reasons for people not being healed. I would like to share these two reasons with you.

Deliberate and Active Unbelief

The first reason people do not receive their healing is because of **deliberate and active unbelief.**

Matthew 13:54-58 (NAS)

And coming to His home town He began teaching them in their synagogue, so that they became astonished, and said, "Where did this man get this wisdom, and these miraculous powers? Is not this the carpenter's son? Is not His mother called Mary, and His brothers, James and Joseph and Simon and Judas? And His sisters, are they not all with us? Where then did this man get all these things [power and authority]*?" And they took offense at Him. But Jesus said to them, "A prophet is not without honor except in his home town, and in his own household." And He did not do many miracles there because of their unbelief.*

Notice that the people of that town recognized His power, His authority, and His wisdom, but they **chose not to believe Him.** Because of that choice, the Bible says He could do no mighty miracles there.

Believing is a choice, and these people chose not to believe. God does not force His will or His gifts on anyone. Therefore, **what we choose to believe will determine what we receive.**

Let's look at what God has to say about believing or not believing:

Mark 16:15-18 (NIV)

> *"Go into all the world and preach the good news to all creation. Whoever believes* [chooses to believe] *and is baptized will be saved, but whoever does not believe* [chooses not to believe] *will be condemned. And these signs will accompany those who believe* [choose to believe]*: In My name they will drive out demons; they will speak in new tongues; they will pick up snakes with their hands; and when they drink deadly poison, it will not hurt them at all; they will place their hands on sick people, and they will get well."*

We all know that these scriptures are talking to the church, but I want you to notice what verses 15 and 16 are saying to us. They say that we, the church, will preach the gospel (Good News), but that some people will choose not to believe our preaching. You see, we cannot make people believe. They must choose to believe or not to believe. Notice the results of their choices. If they choose to believe, they will be saved and forgiven of their sins. But if they choose not to believe, they will be condemned to hell. **The choices they make bring their results.** It is also our choice to believe what God's Word says or not to believe it. We also get the results of our choices.

If we follow the same line of thought in verses 17 and 18 that was shown to us in verses 15 and 16, the verses would read this way:

Those who have chosen to believe will pick up snakes, and if they drink any deadly poison it will not hurt them.

Those who have chosen not to believe must be very careful what they pick up and what they drink, because it could kill them.

Those who have chosen to believe will drive out demons.

Those who have chosen not to believe will not drive out demons, but the demons may drive them out.

Acts 19:13-16 (NIV)

> *Some Jews who went around driving out evil spirits tried to invoke the name of the Lord Jesus over those who were demon-possessed. They would say, "In the name of Jesus, whom Paul preaches, I command you to come out." Seven sons of Sceva, a Jewish chief priest, were doing this. The evil spirit answered them, "Jesus I know, and I know about Paul, but who are you?" Then the man who had the evil spirit jumped on them and overpowered them all. He gave them such a beating that they ran out of the house naked and bleeding.*

The seven sons of Sceva tried to cast out demons in the name of Jesus about whom Paul preached, but the evil spirits jumped on them, overpowered them, and ran them off. Some people tell me they do not believe in demons, but that does not change the fact that demons do exist. Some people do not believe in God, but He still exists.

Those who have chosen to believe will speak in new tongues and become strong. When you pray in the Holy Spirit, you will be built up, edified, and strengthened (see Jude 20, AMP).

Those who have chosen not to believe will not speak in new tongues and will remain weak. According to God's Word, they may be Christians, but they will be weak Christians with little power. The Bible says that **power comes when you pray in tongues.**

Those who have chosen to believe will lay hands on the sick and they will get well.

Those who have chosen not to believe will not lay hands on the sick. Therefore, many of the sick will not get well.

REMEMBER—BELIEVING IS A CHOICE!!

Lack of Knowledge

The second reason people do not receive their healing is because of a **lack of knowledge.**

Hosea 4:6

My people are destroyed for lack of knowledge.

Notice that God said, **"My children,"** not "the world's children." He is talking about believers —Christians. He also said they had a lack of knowledge. For there to be a lack of knowledge there must first be knowledge. The knowledge is the Word of God, and God's Word is **truth.** It is our only source for learning **God's will** and **God's direction** for our lives.

John 8:31,32

If ye continue in my word, then are ye my disciples indeed; and ye shall know the ***truth****, and the* ***truth*** *shall make you free.*

Knowing and choosing to believe God's Word about healing will free you from sickness and disease. Hallelujah!

God's Word gives direction:

Psalm 119:105 (NIV)

Your Word is a lamp to my feet and a light for my path.

God's Word brings healing and deliverance:

Psalm 107:20 (NAS)

He sent His Word and healed them, and delivered them from their destructions.

Proverbs 4:20-22 (NAS)

My son, give attention to my words; Incline your ear to my sayings. Do not let them depart from your sight; Keep them in the midst of your heart. For they are life to those who find them, and health to all their whole body.

As you can see, God's Word should hold a very high place in our lives. It is by His Word that we are born again, and it is by His Word that we are healed. God's Word brings deliverance to the captive and peace to the believer's mind. **Have you chosen to believe God's Word?**

I was not raised in a Christian home, and because of this, I did not know about the love of God. I did not know that my sins could be forgiven and that Jesus paid the price for my body to be healed. When I was born again, I needed healing very badly, because I had many physical problems. By the time I turned twenty-one years old, I had undergone a double hernia operation and two back operations, and both of my feet and knees had been operated on. At seventeen years of age, I found that I had sugar diabetes and epilepsy. I had three or four seizures a day. Just before my twenty-second birthday, I had my third heart attack. As you can see, **my lack of knowledge was killing me.**

I will not take the time to tell you all the things that occurred for me to be born again or that led to my body being healed of those things I just named. But I will say that if it had not been for a stubborn friend who kept inviting me to go to church with him, I probably never would have found that I could be forgiven of my sins or that my body could be healed.

The key to all of the healing I have experienced is that I began studying the Bible for myself to find out the truth of what God and His Son Jesus had done for me. Because of all the different stories and theories I had heard about God, I was confused about many things. I wanted to know the truth, and I realized that I had to find this truth for myself. You cannot live on someone else's faith—you must build your own faith in God.

Mark 4:24 (AMP)

He said to them, Be careful what you are hearing. The measure [of thought and study] you give [to the truth you hear] will be the measure [of virtue and knowledge] that comes back to you—and more [besides] will be given to you who hear.

Remember, **faith will come to you, when YOU hear God's Word**—not when someone else hears God's Word for you.

II

THREE RESPONSIBILITIES FOR RECEIVING YOUR HEALING

Some people are healed by my faith or someone else's faith, but my experience has been that these same people often lose their healing. Other people are always hoping to be healed, but they are never healed because they are waiting on God to make them receive healing. God has already done all that He is going to do to provide for your healing. He gave His Son to pay the price for your healing. Some people simply cannot see past their sickness so that they might receive their healing.

I am often asked if there is something people can do to help them receive and keep their healing. There is. But there are also responsibilities that go along with receiving your healing.

Most people do not like to hear the word **responsibility** because that means *they must do something*. We must remember that God has done all that He will ever do in the matter of providing healing. He gave His only Son on the cross to pay our sin AND our healing. He offers us **salvation**, which includes our **physical** h... Our responsibility is to accept the gift God offers to us.

Isaiah 53:5 (NIV)

But he was pierced for our transgressions, he was crushed for our iniquities; the punishment that brought us peace was upon him and by his wounds [stripes] *we are healed.*

As we can plainly see in these verses, Jesus took upon himself all of our sins, all of our sicknesses, and all which was needful for us to have peace of mind. He paid the supreme price that we could be forgiven of our sins and that we could be healed in our bodies. He gave himself completely for us—spirit, soul, and body—that we might be made whole in our bodies, as well as in our spirits and souls. Since Jesus paid the **complete price** for these things, it is not necessary that we pay the price again. Our responsibility is simply to believe and receive the gift for which Jesus has already paid.

We know that we cannot buy salvation and healing. If that were possible, all the rich people would be saved and free of sickness. But many rich people are on their way to hell because they have not accepted Jesus as their Savior. And many rich people are sick and dying...just like the poor.

As the title of this section suggests, I believe we have three responsibilities in the area of healing:

1. We have the responsibility to **prepare** to receive our healing.
2. We have the responsibility to **receive** our healing.
3. We have the responsibility to **keep** our healing.

I'm sorry to say that most people do not prepare for their healing. They just hope they will be one of the "lucky ones" who gets healed, and there is no preparation on their part to receive their healing.

As I mentioned earlier, some people receive their healing by my faith or someone else's faith, but because they do not know how to keep their healing, they often lose it. This should not be so. If God gives us something, we should be able to keep it. How would you feel if you had gone to the jewelry store, bought me the most expensive watch in the store, gave it to me, and I lost it the very first day? You would not be very happy, would you? How do you think God feels when He gave us a gift that cost the most precious thing He possessed—His only Son—and then we lose it?

When people lose their healing, they usually say, "I thought I got healed, but I guess I really didn't." Others blame God for losing their healing ...or they blame the preacher, saying his prayers were not strong enough. Seldom do they look at themselves and ask, **"What am I doing wrong?"** But in order to have a successful healing experience, we must accept some of the responsibility ourselves.

III

PREPARE TO RECEIVE YOUR HEALING

I have found there to be only two causes for sickness. The first cause is our own *stupidity*. We cannot blame God—or the devil—if we go out in the cold improperly dressed and then get sick. That is our fault. Because of our foolishness, we are sick. We cannot blame God—or the devil—if we smoke, drink, overeat, or do anything else that is harmful to our bodies, causing sickness or even death. But we can believe God to forgive us for doing these things, and believe Him to heal our bodies of the results of this foolishness. Now, I do not advocate becoming a health food or fitness "nut," but we do need to use some godly wisdom in these areas of our lives.

The second cause for sickness is *sin*. Now, listen to me before you run off and tell someone that Billy Smith said he is sick because he has sin in his life. That is not what I am saying! Some sicknesses are caused by sin in our personal lives. Other sicknesses are due to the fact that sin is present in the world. A baby who gets AIDS from a drug-addict parent did not get sick because of his own sin. This sickness resulted from the sin in the world. We understand through God's Word that sin came into the world through the downfall of Adam and Eve. From that point on, the Bible records many instances of sickness, disease, and death.

James 5:14,15

> *Is any sick among you? let him call for the elders of the church; and let them pray over him, anointing him with oil in the name of the Lord: And the prayer of faith shall save the sick, and the Lord shall raise him up; and* ***if he have committed sins****, they shall be forgiven him.*

I have been praying for the sick for over twenty years. I have found that the two most common causes for sickness are **unforgiveness and bitterness (sin)**. I have talked to doctors in forty different countries and most of them agree with me. I have found that many joint problems, such as arthritis and bursitis, and many other physical problems, are caused by unforgiveness and bitterness.

I also believe that **unforgiveness and bitterness** are the two greatest hindrances to keeping your healing.

Paul, writing to the Ephesians, tells them to release all wrath, envy, jealousy, slander, and many other things which go along with unforgiveness and bitterness. I believe this is because of the damage that is done to both the body and spirit when we hold on to these things.

Ephesians 4:31,32 (NAS)

Let all bitterness and wrath and anger and clamor and slander be put away from you, along with all malice. And be kind to one another, tenderhearted, forgiving each other, just as God in Christ also has forgiven you.

Here are a few more scriptures that show some of the problems caused by sin:

Proverbs 14:30 (NIV)

A heart at peace gives life to the body, but envy rots the bones.

Proverbs 15:13 (NIV)

A happy heart makes the face cheerful, but heartache crushes the spirit.

Proverbs 17:22 (NIV)

A cheerful heart is good medicine, but a crushed spirit dries up the bones.

Proverbs 18:14 (NAS)

The spirit of a man can endure his sickness, but a broken spirit who can bear?

Just as evil words and deeds bring sickness, physically and spiritually, so good words and deeds bring health, physically and spiritually.

Proverbs 15:30 (NIV)

A cheerful look brings joy to the heart, and good news gives health to the bones.

Proverbs 16:24 (NIV)

Pleasant words are a honeycomb, sweet to the soul and healing to the bones.

I have never found a tumor in the breast area that was not caused by bitterness. I make this statement because I have prayed for thousands of people with tumors in the breast area. When I deal with the unforgiveness and bitterness, the tumors always dissolve.

Ecclesiastes 7:9 (NAS)

Do not be eager in your heart to be angry, for anger resides in the bosom [breast] *of fools.*

I believe anger is the seed. This is why Paul said, "Don't let the sun go down on your anger... don't let bitterness take root in you." Anger is the seed. As we meditate on this seed (talk about it, worry about it, think about it), the seed of anger begins to take root and grows from anger to bitterness.

People often tell me, "I will forgive them, but I will never forget what they have done." **I tell them**

that we must not only forgive, but we must do as God has done, and also forget. God has placed our sins in a place of forgetfulness where He never remembers them again. He says that our sins have been separated from us *as far as the east is from the west* (Psalm 103:12).

Isaiah 43:25

> *I, even I, am he that blotteth out thy transgressions for mine own sake, and will not remember thy sins.*

Matthew 6:14,15 (NIV)

> *For if you forgive men when they sin against you, your heavenly Father will also forgive you. But if you do not forgive men their sins, your Father will not forgive your sins.*

Many people tell me, **"You don't know what they did to me."** That is true. I do not know what they did to you, but I can see and hear what unforgiveness and bitterness are doing to you. It is not worth holding on to the past. **We must see that it is in the past. We can do nothing to change the fact that it happened, but we can change our future by releasing our past.**

Philippians 3:13,14

> *Brethren, I count not myself to have apprehended: but this one thing I do, forgetting those things which are behind, and reaching forth unto those things which are before, I*

press toward the mark for the prize of the high calling of God in Christ Jesus.

Isaiah 43:18 (NAS)

"Do not call to mind the former things, or ponder things of the past."

Paul tells us that we are to release the past and the things that come from the past. It is our choice to do these things. It is simply an act of our will! Remember—

Ephesians 4:31,32 (NAS)

Let all bitterness and wrath and anger and clamor and slander be put away from you, along with all malice. And be kind to one another, tenderhearted, forgiving each other, just as God in Christ also has forgiven you.

But how can we forget these things?

I can tell you from my own personal experience that if you will pray for those who have hurt you, you can forgive them. You cannot pray for someone very long and still manage to hold on to bitterness and unforgiveness.

Luke 6:27,28

But I say unto you which hear, Love your enemies, do good to them which hate you, bless them that curse you, and pray for them which despitefully use you.

1. I must first ask God to forgive me for allowing bitterness to take root in my life.

2. Then I must ask God to forgive the person who has hurt me.

I can do this when I recognize that this person is not my enemy. The one who has deceived them—Satan—is my enemy. I must realize that I, too, have probably allowed Satan to use me to hurt others in some way. Then I must recognize that I cannot do this in my own flesh. I can only do this by the Spirit of God.

Ephesians 6:12

For we wrestle not against flesh and blood, but against principalities, against powers, against the rulers of the darkness of this world, against spiritual wickedness in high places.

2 Corinthians 10:3-5 (NAS)

For though we walk in the flesh, we do not war according to the flesh, for the weapons of our warfare are not of the flesh, but divinely powerful for the destruction of fortresses. We are destroying speculations and every lofty thing raised up against the knowledge of God, and we are taking every thought captive to the obedience of Christ.

3. Next, if the person does not know Jesus as their Savior, I must pray for their salvation. I must ask God to send the right person to witness to them, and pray that their eyes and heart will be open to the gospel.

I have never found a Christian who wants anyone to go to hell. Sometimes they may want God to punish others for what they have done, but they do not want to see them go to hell. Praying for those who have hurt us will cause blessings to come to us.

1 Peter 3:9,10

Not rendering evil for evil, or railing for railing: but contrariwise blessing; knowing that ye are thereunto called, that ye should inherit a blessing. For he that will love life, and see good days, let him refrain his tongue from evil, and his lips that they speak no guile.

Romans 12:21 (NAS)

Do not be overcome by evil, but overcome evil with good.

The first thing we must do in preparation for our healing is to judge ourselves according to God's Word to see if we have sin in our lives. God's Word says our spirit will tell us if we have sinned. If our heart (our spirit) does not condemn us, then we are not condemned. But if we have allowed sin to come into our lives, then all we have to do is confess our sin, and it will be forgiven—as if we never did it in the first place.

1 John 1:9 (NAS)

If we confess our sins, He is faithful and righteous to forgive us our sins and to cleanse us from all unrighteousness.

We must remember that the Bible tells us to repent of our sins. Repenting means to be sorry for our sins. We must turn and walk away from our old life of sin and start over with a new life. Through the Spirit of the Lord, we can become new creatures.

After we have taken care of any sin problem in our lives, we must go to the next step in preparing for our healing.

Decide That You Want To Be Healed

We must make a choice—to be healed or not to be healed. God does not heal us just because we need healing. He does not force His will on us. We must choose to accept His gift of healing.

People say to me all the time, "No one would choose not to be healed if they could be, would they?"

Recognize this: We are not talking about believing or not believing—we are talking about wanting to be healed or not wanting to be healed. There is a difference. I would like to tell you about some people who chose not to be healed and why they made that choice.

At one of our street meetings in Graz, Austria, we shared the love of Jesus, telling the people that He was still healing the sick today. An elderly woman crippled with arthritis came forward. We told her that Jesus would heal her. She said, "I am a Catholic." I said, "That is all right. God heals Catholics, too." I explained about healing, and then I prayed for her. She was miraculously healed.

I noticed a crippled man who was watching closely and I walked over to him and asked if he had seen what happened to this woman. He said he had seen her being healed. Then I asked him if he believed God could heal him, too. He said he did. I asked him if he wanted me to pray for him, and he said, **"No!"** I asked him why he did not want me to pray if he believed God could heal him. This is what he told me:

> Twenty years ago, I jumped out of a plane. My parachute did not open until just before I hit the ground. I broke my back in two places, and I broke both of my knees. If I got healed now, I would lose my pension.

I have ministered to other people—deaf, blind, or crippled—who are afraid to be healed. They have learned to function in life the way they are, and they are afraid to change. If they were healed, they would have to learn to live a whole different way of life, and that scares them.

Then there are always those who would have nothing to talk about if they were healed. Every time you get around them, they tell you about every ache and pain they have had for the last twenty years. This is their way of getting attention, so they do not want to be healed. Even though some of them come in the prayer line for healing, they do not receive it. God knows their hearts and He will not force healing on those who really do not want it.

You see, there are those who do not want to be healed. And for whatever reason—**the choice is theirs.**

Does God Want Everyone To Be Healed?

In preparing to be healed, I had to find out if it was really God's will to heal everyone. God is moved by faith in His Word, and you cannot have faith to believe for what you do not know. So I had to know the truth for myself.

I had been told many things that were not true about healing:

- Some people told me that God was not healing anyone today.
- Others said God wanted to heal some people but not others.

- Then there were those who said God puts sickness on some people to either punish them or teach them a lesson.

All of these things could not be true. The day I gave my life to Jesus, my pastor did something that changed my whole life. He gave me a Bible and told me to read it. He said it was a personal letter to me from God.

I decided that if I wanted to know what God thought about healing, I should read what He had written to me in the Bible. Surely if I read what God had said, then I would know His will.

John 8:31,32

If ye ***continue in my word****, then are ye my disciples indeed; and ye shall know the* ***truth****, and the* ***truth*** *shall make you free.*

As I began to read the Bible, I found that healing was mentioned throughout the Bible—in the Old Testament as well as the New Testament. While reading the Bible, I discovered two scriptures that really excited me:

Hebrews 13:8 (NAS)

Jesus Christ is the same yesterday and today, yes and forever.

This means that if He healed yesterday, He will heal today. And if He heals today, then He will also heal tomorrow.

Acts 10:34

Then Peter opened his mouth, and said, Of a truth I perceive that God is no respecter of persons.

Look at what these two scriptures are saying. If Jesus has ever healed anyone, He will heal us, for He is no respecter of people. What He has done for them, He will do for us! Praise God!

What is God's will regarding healing?
We find in the Old Testament:

Isaiah 53:5 (NIV)

But he was pierced for our transgressions, he was crushed for our iniquities; the punishment that brought us peace was upon him, and by his wounds [stripes] *we are healed.*

This scripture tells us that Jesus paid the price for our sins and that when we are forgiven, fear and worry can no longer steal our peace. It also says that by the wounds (stripes) He received, we can be healed. This scripture clearly shows that God intends for us to be made complete—spirit, soul, and body.

Notice that all of these things are listed in the **same scripture**. The price that Jesus paid for forgiveness of our sins also included our peace of mind and our physical healing.

John 3:16,17 (NAS)

"For God so loved the world, that He gave His only begotten Son, that whoever believes in Him should not perish, but have eternal life. For God did not send the Son into the world to judge the world, but that the world should be saved through Him."

All of us believe this means that the whole world can be saved or forgiven of their sins. When I make this statement, people have no problem believing it. But if I say that God also wants the whole world to be healed, some people will get very angry with me because they know someone who did not get healed. We all know people who are not born again, but that does not change the fact that God still wants everyone to be born again. Mark 16:15,16 says we are to tell the Good News, but it also says that some people will choose not to believe it.

There are several scriptures that show us God's will regarding healing:

Psalm 103:1-3 (NAS)

Bless the Lord, O my soul; and all that is within me, bless His holy name. Bless the Lord, O my soul, and forget none of His benefits; who pardons all your iniquities; who heals all your diseases.

This is David talking to us—telling us that there are benefits to serving God. **The results of serving God are forgiveness of sin and healing of the**

body. All through the Old Testament, you will find Israel turning away from God to serve other gods, and sickness is one of the results of this sin. But as soon as Israel turned back to God, healing took place.

Even in the Old Testament, God was no respecter of people. Whoever came to Him, Jew or Gentile, was healed. And it made no difference how many people came to Him—one or a million—He healed them all.

In 2 Kings 5:1-27, Naaman, the commander of the army of Aram, went to Elisha, the prophet of God, and was healed of leprosy.

In Psalm 105:37, when Israel came out of bondage from Egypt, God healed them all. It is estimated that there were between two and three million people healed at one time.

Psalm 105:37

He brought them forth also with silver and gold: and there was not one feeble person among their tribes.

In the New Testament, the same thing took place, as people came to Jesus for healing. It made no difference if there was one person on the side of the road or if there was a whole village—Jesus healed them all.

Mark 10:46-52 says that Jesus stopped on the side of the road to heal a blind beggar named Bartimaeus. In Matthew 9:35, Jesus went about in all the cities and villages, healing every kind of disease and every kind of sickness.

Matthew 9:35 (NAS)

And Jesus was going about all the cities and the villages, teaching in their synagogues, and proclaiming the gospel of the kingdom, and healing every kind of disease and every kind of sickness.

God wants to heal some people, but He does not want to heal others.

This statement has caused many people not to seek healing. Because the devil has given them such a low opinion of themselves, they think God doesn't want to heal them. **If you believe this statement, the devil will always tell you that you are the one God does not want to heal.** This is not true.

You cannot find any place in the Old or New Testament where any person or group of people came to God or Jesus for healing and did not get healed. **It has always been the will of God for us to be healed.**

Sickness Is Not Judgment or Punishment of Sin

God's judgment for sin is hell—not sickness and disease, and poverty and calamity. Satan is the god of this world, and he is the author of sickness, disease, poverty, calamity, and death. These conditions are the result of sin, and the only way out is through the blood of Jesus and the Word of God. Remember—

John 3:16,17 (NAS)

"For God so loved the world, that He gave His only begotten Son, that whoever believes in Him should not perish, but have eternal life. For God did not send the Son into the world to judge the world, but that the world should be saved through Him."

As we can see by this scripture, Jesus did not come into the world to judge the world of its sin. He came to save the world from its sin and from the results of sin. When you look up the word **saved**, you will find that it means "to be made whole, spiritually, mentally, and physically."

Deuteronomy 28:1-14 says if we hear and obey God, all of His blessings will be upon us. We will be blessed in the city and in the field. We will be blessed in our body and in the bodies of our children. We will also be blessed in our land and in the animals of our land. We will be blessed in everything we do. But if we choose to disobey God and His Word, we will walk in the curses of sin. We will be cursed in all of the above-named blessings.

Psalm 91:1-16 says if we place ourselves under the covering of God, He will protect us from every sickness and disease and from every plague that would come near us or our household. It also says that we shall have long lives—we will live until we are satisfied with our lives.

James 1:17

Every good gift and every perfect gift is from above, and cometh down from the Father of lights, with whom is no variableness, neither shadow of turning.

Sickness and disease, and poverty and calamity are not good and perfect gifts. If these were good, we would not go to the doctor to get well or to the banker to borrow money. Instead, we would receive them with great joy.

God's desire for our lives is that we prosper and be in health.

3 John 2 (NAS)

Beloved, I pray that in all respects you may prosper and be in good health, just as your soul prospers.

God's perfect will for us is that we prosper and be in health, spiritually, mentally, and physically.

If God does not put sickness and disease and all of these other bad things on us, where do they come from? That is a good question and the answer is found in God's own Word.

John 10:10 (NAS)

"The thief [Satan], *comes only to steal, and kill, and destroy; I came that they might have life, and might have it abundantly."*

Again I say that sickness and disease or any of the other bad things I have mentioned are not abundant life. That is why Jesus healed the woman who had been crippled—by Satan—for eighteen long years.

Luke 13:16 (NIV)

"Then should not this woman, a daughter of Abraham, whom Satan has kept bound for eighteen long years, be set free on the Sabbath day from what bound her?"

God does not teach by sickness, poverty, and calamity.

Some people say that when a child dies, God is trying to teach the parents something. That doesn't teach the parents anything—except to hate God for taking their child. I have also heard people say that God teaches us to be humble through poverty. That does not teach us anything. People will do whatever it takes to meet the needs of their families, even if it means they have to steal.

I can find only one scriptural way that God teaches us anything, and that is **by His Word, through the Holy Spirit.**

John 14:23-26 (NAS)

"If anyone loves Me, he will keep My word; and My Father will love him, and We will come to him and make Our abode with him. He who does not love Me does not keep My

words; and the word which you hear is not Mine, but the Father's who sent Me. These things I have spoken to you, while abiding with you. But the Helper, ***the Holy Spirit,*** *whom the Father will send in My name, He* ***will teach you all things****, and bring to your remembrance all that I said to you."*

Now that we have established that God wants everyone to be healed and that He does not put sickness and disease on people to teach them something or to punish them, let's find out how we can receive our healing.

Faith Moves God

God does not move just because we have a need in our lives. God moves when we release faith in His Word.

Hebrews 11:6 (NAS)

And without faith it is impossible to please Him, for he who comes to God must believe that ***He is****, and that He is* ***a rewarder*** *of those who seek Him.*

If we cannot please God without faith, then how do we get faith? God provides faith through His Word, because faith comes from hearing His Word.

Romans 10:17

So then faith cometh by hearing, and hearing by the Word of God.

I have had people tell me that their faith was built up from listening to others give their testimony of what God had done for them or that their faith was built up from their past experiences with God. These statements sound good, but they do not agree with what God said. He said, **"Faith comes by hearing the Word of God."**

Our faith is not built up by hearing the testimonies of others. However, our faith—gained from hearing God's Word—is stirred up by hearing the testimonies of what God has done for others. Our experiences do not build our faith—our experiences confirm our faith in God's Word. Because of our faith in God's Word, we are able to share many wonderful experiences.

Let me emphasize that I am not saying you should stop reading your Bible and memorizing scriptures—these things also play a part in our healing and in our faith. But faith comes when we hear God's Word down in our spirits and not up in our heads. When faith comes, we put action to our prayers.

As we hear the promises of God in His Word, faith will rise in us to receive these promises. It is God's Word that saves us, heals us, and delivers us from the destroyer—Satan.

Psalm 107:20 (NAS)

He sent His word and healed them, and delivered them from their destructions.

We must realize that the Word was Jesus. They are one and the same. God the Father sent Him to free us from Satan and his destroying power.

John 1:1-5,14 (NAS)

In the beginning was the Word, and the Word was with God, ***and the Word was God.***
He was in the beginning with God.
All things came into being by Him, and apart from Him nothing came into being that has come into being.
In Him was life, and the life was the light of men.
And the light shines in the darkness, and the darkness did not comprehend it.
And the Word became flesh, and dwelt among us, and we beheld His glory, glory as of the only begotten from the Father, full of grace and truth.

We still have the written Word of God with us today, and that written Word is just as powerful as if Jesus were here speaking them out loud. The Bible tells us that His Words are never-ending, and that His Words will not come back empty. His Words are life.

Matthew 24:35 (NAS)

"Heaven and earth will pass away, but My words shall not pass away."

Isaiah 55:11 (NAS)

"So shall My word be which goes forth from My mouth; it shall not return to Me empty, without accomplishing what I desire, and without succeeding in the matter for which I sent it."

Some people say, "If Jesus was only here I could be healed." But listen to what Jesus has to say about His Word.

John 6:62,63 (NAS)

"What then if you should behold the Son of Man ascending where He was before? It is the Spirit who gives life; the flesh profits nothing; the words that I have spoken to you are spirit and are life."

The Word of God is the most important thing we have on the earth. As I have already stated, it is God's Word that saves us, and it is His Word that delivers us and heals us.

We are born again by the Word of God:

1 Peter 1:23 (NAS)

For you have been born again not of seed which is perishable but imperishable, that is, through the living and abiding word of God.

God's Word keeps us from sin:

Psalm 119:9 (NAS)

How can a young man keep his way pure? By keeping it according to Thy word.

Psalm 119:11 (NAS)

Thy Word I have treasured in my heart, that I may not sin against Thee.

God's Word brings deliverance:

Psalm 119:170 (NAS)

Let my supplication come before Thee; Deliver me according to Thy word.

God's Word brings healing:

Psalm 107:20 (NAS)

He sent His word and healed them, and delivered them from their destructions.

Remember that Romans 10:17 says, *faith cometh by hearing...the Word of God.* It does not say that faith comes from simply reading the Word of God. I know many people who have read the Word of God over and over, but they have no faith. I know many people who have memorized God's Word, but they have no faith.

Faith does not come by memorizing God's Word or just by reading it. It simply comes by hearing God's Word. That is why I tell people, "When you read God's Word, read it out loud." They often ask me, "What will people think if I read out loud?" Who cares? The important thing is that when you are obedient to do what God's Word says, **you will be healed**.

I remind you again that reading the Word quietly and memorizing scriptures are important study methods, and we should use them. But **hearing** the Word of God is what produces faith.

I am not saying that just hearing with your ears will bring healing. You must let the words go past your mind—into your spirit. Until the message gets into your spirit, it will not become faith. The path to your spirit begins in the ears and goes through the mind. We cannot let the Word stop in our minds—we must meditate or speak God's Word into our spirits. We must understand that God does not put anything in the Bible just to fill up space. If something is in the Bible, it is there for us to hear and obey. If we do that, we will receive the results that His Word promises.

God's Word must be personal.

I find that most Christians read the Bible for other people. The husband reads the Bible for his wife, so he can point out what she is doing wrong. And the wife does the same for her husband. The church member is reading the Word of God to find out what the other members are doing wrong or what the pastor is doing wrong. Some people read the Bible to find out what someone else needs to be doing in order to receive healing...but they run to the doctor for their own healing. **Until your Bible reading becomes PERSONAL, you will never be able to receive from God.**

Hear God's Word Regarding Healing

If you need healing, the most important thing you can do is to hear what God's Word has to say about it. When you need healing, you don't need to hear what God's Word says about prophecy or deliverance—you need to read and hear what it says about healing. If you need healing, then find scriptures on healing and begin reading them out loud. Use both the eye gate and the ear gate. But remember—**faith comes from hearing God's Word.**

What you listen to is vital to your healing. If you listen to people who tell you that God is not healing today, then eventually you will believe that. If you listen to those who say you are nobody and will never amount to anything, then you will have a hard time believing that you can be healed. If all you hear is that you are going to die because you have cancer, you probably will, because you do not know that you can be healed.

Mark 4:24 (AMP)

Be careful what you are hearing. The measure [of thought and study] you give [to the truth you hear] will be the measure [of virtue and knowledge] that comes back to you—and more [besides] will be given to you who hear.

I believe this next scripture is the most important scripture you can read regarding healing. If you can get this word into your spirit and begin to act on it, healing is guaranteed.

Proverbs 4:20-22 (NAS)

My son, give attention to my words; incline your ear to my sayings.
Do not let them depart from your sight; keep them in the midst of your heart.
For they are life to those who find them, and health to all their whole body.

Look at what this scripture is saying. If we hear God's Word, it will become health to our whole body. It does not say that the first time we hear God's Word it will become health to our whole body. But as we hear it...and hear it again...it will become faith. Faith will become reality, and **we will be healed!**

Because of this scripture, I have written a small pocket-size book entitled ***Health—a Gift of God.*** This book is full of scriptures on healing. I start the book by asking the question, "Is it God's will for all to be healed?" Then I answer this question with God's Word—not with my opinion. Next I ask the question, "If it is God's will for all to be healed, then why isn't everyone healed?" Again I answer this question with nothing but scripture. The rest of the book is scripture after scripture about healing, because faith comes from hearing...and hearing... God's Word (see Romans 10:17).

I want to share with you again the two scriptures that helped me see that it really is God's will for anyone and everyone to be healed. **Catch hold of these powerful verses.**

Hebrews 13:8 (NAS)

Jesus Christ is the same yesterday and today, yes and forever.

Acts 10:34 (NAS)

Peter said: "I most certainly understand now that God is not one to show partiality."

As we read and hear what God has done for others, our faith in His Word will begin to rise up so that we may receive our healing.

Probably the most important piece of material this ministry has ever put out to help people prepare for their healing is an audiotape entitled **"Health—a Gift of God."** It is identical to the mini-book, but it must be listened to.

God's Word is like a medicine. We must take it regularly for it to do us any good. If the doctor tells you to take your medicine twice a day and you only take it once every two days, it will do you no good because you didn't follow the instructions. It is just as important to hear God's Word. That is the only way it can become health to your whole body.

When I put this tape out, I did not realize the impact it would have on people with incurable diseases. People who had cancer, multiple sclerosis, and many other incurable diseases, were healed simply because they listened to this tape. They listened to it over and over until they were healed and pronounced well by the doctors.

This Is Your Prescription

1. If you are not sick, listen to this tape at least once a week. (This is called preventive medicine.)
2. If you are sick, listen to this tape every day.
3. If you are sick sick (if you have a cold you are sick, but if you have cancer, you are sick sick), you need to soak yourself in this tape—if possible, listen to it night and day.

I have found that the best time to listen to this tape is at night when you are asleep. During the daytime there are so many interruptions. Put the tape in your walkman at night and go to sleep. The message will go straight into your spirit.

Some who have soaked themselves in this tape have had healing manifested within three days. No one I know of has listened for more than three months without being healed.

Let me say that it is much easer to build your faith before a storm hits than after. In fact, **it is almost impossible to build your faith in the middle of a storm.** This is because most people get caught up in the storm instead of in the answer. But **any-**

one who puts God's Word into action will see his/her circumstances changed. Prepare now to receive.

IV

RECEIVE YOUR HEALING

Now that **faith has come**, we must remember that ***faith without works is dead*** (James 2:20).

James 2:17 (NIV)

Faith by itself, if it is not accompanied by action, is dead.

When we have studied and meditated on God's Word, **faith will come**, but that does not mean that we will automatically receive from God. You see, we still have the choice to believe faith or to believe our body, mind, or the situation. Remember—we must choose to believe, and what we choose to believe will determine what we receive.

Faith says, "You can move mountains." (See Matthew 17:20.)
Your body says, "You're too weak."
Your mind says, "That is right. Let someone else do it."

Faith says, "You can do all things through Christ Jesus." (See Philippians 4:13.)
Your mind says, "You know you cannot do anything. You're not as good as they are."
Your body says, "That is right. Just sit down and rest."

Faith says, "You are healed by the stripes Jesus bore." (See Isaiah 53:5.)
Your body says, "You do not feel healed."
Your mind says, "Well, if you do not feel healed, then you probably are not healed."

We must decide if we will believe faith, which is God's Word, or if we will believe our symptoms and situations. It is our responsibility to line up our minds and bodies with the Word of God.

Romans 12:1,2

I beseech you therefore, brethren, by the mercies of God, that ye present your bodies a living sacrifice, holy, acceptable unto God, which is your reasonable service. And be not conformed to this world: but be ye transformed by the renewing of your mind, that ye may prove what is that good, and acceptable, and perfect, will of God.

It has been my experience that most people are waiting on God to heal them. I hear this statement over and over: "One of these days God will heal me." We must recognize that according to God's Word, **He has already healed us.**

1 Peter 2:24 (NAS)

He Himself bore our sins in His body on the cross, that we might die to sin and live to righteousness; for by His wounds [stripes] *you were healed.*

Notice that everything this scripture is talking about is written in the past tense. It has already taken place. He paid the price for our sins to be forgiven, but until we accept that fact, we are not made righteous. Likewise, until we accept the fact that He paid the price for our healing, we will not be healed.

Many times I literally have to walk people through to their healing, scripture by scripture—taking them step by step through what Jesus did for them. When I do this, most of them receive their healing. Still, a few people say, "I just cannot believe it." Or they say, "That is just too easy." But it is still true, and **God will not force anyone to be healed.**

A few years ago I was in Romania, ministering in a church where many deaf people attended. That city was the home of a school for the deaf. Deaf students from all over Romania attended there. One day as I ministered to the people, many who were partially deaf, as well as those who were totally deaf, waited for prayer in the prayer line. There were five people who were both deaf and dumb. As I began to pray, I noticed that there seemed to be a strong anointing for the healing of deafness that night. We were seeing each one healed as we prayed. Then I prayed for the first deaf and dumb person, and he was healed. I prayed for a few more people, and then I came to the second deaf and dumb person. When I prayed, nothing happened.

This sometimes happens when I am praying for people, and I have learned not to let it bother me. I just sat the man down and, through an interpreter, I told him to watch as others were being healed. This sometimes causes an individual's faith to rise to the point where they can receive healing.

I prayed for several more people, and then I came to the third deaf and dumb person. I prayed for her and she was healed. She could hear and speak. I called the deaf man back up, and he asked her if she could hear and speak. She told him, "Yes." I prayed for him and again he received nothing. Again I told him to sit down and watch others who were being healed. As I continued praying for folks, they were all healed, including the other two who were deaf and dumb. However, this one man still did not receive his healing.

I had sat him down for the fourth time when I heard God say, "Would you like to know why he is not receiving his healing?" I said, "Yes." God said, "He is waiting for Me to push healing on him." I asked God, "What do You mean?"

This is how God explained it to me. He said, "You can take the book you have in your hand and offer it to someone as a gift. You can hold it out for them to take or you can leave it for them at the front of the church. But until they reach out and pick it up, it is just a gift that you have offered to them. It does not become theirs until they reach out and take it."

God told me that He had offered everyone the gift of salvation (see Romans 6:23), but unless they accept it, they will go to hell. God does not force salvation or any other of His gifts on us. He offers us the gift of the Holy Spirit (see Luke 11:13), but unless we accept it, it will not become ours. It is the same way with healing. We must accept the healing He has provided.

After I explained this to the young man, he understood, and he reached out and took his healing from God.

Faith without works is dead.

I often hear people say, "If I am healed, then I will believe." I am sorry, but that is not the way it works. Remember, God moves according to our faith in His Word. We must believe His Word and then the healing (or whatever we are believing God for) will be manifested.

I am no different than many of you. I have the same thoughts that come to you. I sometimes think, "What if it does not work?" Even though I have prayed for thousands of people to be healed, I must believe for my healing just like everyone else.

God's Word says, *Faith without works is dead.* That means it will not work.

James 2:14,17 (NAS)

What use is it, my brethren, if a man says he has faith, but he has no works? Can that faith save him?...Even so faith, if it has no works, is dead, being by itself.

I would like to share a couple of testimonies that will show what I am talking about.

In 1990, when I was in Canada holding a meeting, a man came forward in a wheelchair. He had cancer and the muscles in his back had been removed. He could not walk or stand. I said, "When I pray for you, do something you could not do." I prayed for him and went on to the next person in line. I heard this man say, "I am going to get up." Someone reached to help him and he said, "No. I must do it."

As I watched, he pushed himself out of the wheelchair and stood up. Immediately he fell on his face on the floor. The people reached out to pick him up. He said, "No. Get back!" He again pushed himself up. This time he stood up and walked out of the church—healed. Praise God!

There were several times when someone prayed for me that I did not feel healed, but I would rise up with faith in God's Word and begin to walk. Usually the first step or two would hurt, but as I continued to walk, the healing would be totally manifested.

I want you to understand that I was not denying the fact that I had sickness and pain, but I was denying sickness and pain the right to stay in my body.

I have two scriptures that give me the right to believe this way:

Psalm 56:9 (TLB)

The very day I call for help, the tide of battle turns.

Romans 4:17 (NIV)

As it is written: "I have made you a father of many nations." He is our father in the sight of God, in whom he believed—the God who gives life to the dead and calls things that are not as though they were.

Speak To Your Problem

I read a scripture a few years ago that changed my entire prayer life. I started getting results where I had been getting none. I believe that if you will listen to what I am about to tell you, it will change your prayer life and you will begin to get the results that you have always wanted.

Mark 11:22-24 (NAS)

"Have faith in God. Truly I say to you, whoever says to this mountain, 'Be taken up and cast into the sea,' and does not doubt in his heart, but believes that what he says is going to happen, it shall be granted him. Therefore I say to you, all things for which you pray and ask, believe that you have received them, and they shall be granted you."

As I studied the Word of God, I found that verse 22 should not have read *Have faith in God*, but it should have read, **"Have the God-kind of faith."** Verses 23 and 24 tell us what the God-kind of faith is—it commands, decrees, asks, and receives.

Most people go to God after all else fails, hoping He can do something to help. But the Bible says to seek God first, and all the promises of God will come upon us.

I would like to give you an example of how most Christians pray when they have cancer, or when they are facing bankruptcy or some other disaster. They go to God—crying, screaming, begging, and pleading—and tell Him how bad their circumstances are. They inform Him that if He does not do something quickly, they will die or will lose everything they have. They tell God how big their mountain is. But that is not what God said we should do. He said for us to go to the mountain and to **tell the mountain what to do** or to **tell the mountain how big our God is.** We are to speak to that mountain of sickness or disaster, telling it to line up with God's Word. Because of the price Jesus paid and because of the authority God has given to us through the powerful name of Jesus, we can expect that mountain or problem to line up with God's Word (see Matthew 21:21). Amen!

I am not telling you to deny that you are sick or that you have a problem. I am saying that we must agree with God's Word and, in doing this, we should deny sickness the right to stay in our bodies. We should not allow problems to control our lives.

Romans 4:17 says that God calls those things which be not as though they were. Tell your body to line up with God's Word that says you are healed (see 1 Peter 2:24). Deny your body the right to stay sick, in agreement with the Word of God.

Choose When and How Your Healing Will Come

Until we realize that we choose the time and place of our healing—and even how we are healed—there will be very little change. I find that most people are waiting on God to decide when and how they are to be healed, or they are waiting on Jesus to decide. I want you to know that neither God the Father nor Jesus will make that decision for you. The decision is totally in your hands. You say, "But He is God." Yes, but God the Father and His Son, Jesus, have already done all they will ever do about your sins being forgiven and about your body being healed.

We have three major examples illustrating that we can choose when and how we are to receive our healing. The people in these examples believed that Jesus was who He said He was, and they believed He could do what He said He could do. This is the key: **believe the Word of God.**

We find the first two examples in the same passage of Scripture:

Matthew 9:18-26 (NAS)

While He was saying these things to them, behold, there came a synagogue official, and bowed down before Him, saying, "My daughter has just died; but come and lay Your hand on her, and she will live." And Jesus rose and began to follow him, and so did His disciples.

And behold, a woman who had been suffering from a hemorrhage for twelve years, came up behind Him and touched the fringe of His cloak; for she was saying to herself, "If I only touch His garment, I shall get well." But Jesus turning and seeing her said, "Daughter, take courage; your faith has made you well." And at once the woman was made well.

And when Jesus came into the official's house, and saw the flute-players, and the crowd in noisy disorder, He began to say, "Depart; for the girl has not died, but is asleep." And they began laughing at Him. But when the crowd had been put out, He entered and took her by the hand; and the girl arose. And this news went out into all that land.

Notice that the father said, "My daughter is dead. But if You will come and lay Your hand on her, she shall live." He chose the time and he chose how his daughter was to be healed—**when Jesus laid His hand on her.**

The woman with the issue of blood said to herself, "If I touch His clothes, I will be healed." She pushed through the crowd, touched His clothes, and she was made whole. She chose the time and she chose how she would be healed—**when she touched His clothes.**

The third example is the centurion. Jesus said he had great faith.

Luke 7:2-10 (NAS)

And a certain centurion's slave, who was highly regarded by him, was sick and about to die. And when he heard about Jesus, he sent some Jewish elders asking Him to come and save the life of his slave. And when they had come to Jesus, they earnestly entreated Him, saying, "He is worthy for You to grant this to him; for he loves our nation, and it was he who built us our synagogue."

Now Jesus started on His way with them; and when He was already not far from the house, the centurion sent friends, saying to Him, "Lord, do not trouble Yourself further, for I am not worthy for You to come under my roof; for this reason I did not even consider myself worthy to come to You, but just say the Word, and my servant will be healed. For I, too, am a man under authority, with soldiers under me; and I say to this one, 'Go!' and he goes; and to another, 'Come!'

and he comes; and to my slave, 'Do this!' and he does it."

Now when Jesus heard this, He marveled at him, and turned and said to the multitude that was following Him, "I say to you, not even in Israel have I found such great faith." And when those who had been sent returned to the house, they found the slave in good health.

The centurion simply believed that Jesus was who He said He was—the Son of God. He believed that Jesus had authority over sickness and disease and that all He had to do was speak, and the sickness and disease would obey Him.

Jesus was amazed. He called this the greatest kind of faith. The centurion simply believed the Word of God.

- The synagogue official believed that if Jesus would touch his daughter's hand, she would live—**and she did.**
- The woman with the issue of blood believed that when she touched His clothes, she would be healed—**and she was.**
- The centurion believed that when Jesus spoke, his servant would be healed—**and he was.**

Each one chose the place and how they were to be healed. We must decide when and how we are going to be healed. **Choose your point of contact, and release your faith when that point of contact is made.**

When I lay hands on people, I tell them to let that be their point of contact. At that moment they must release their faith. I join my faith with theirs, and together we receive their healing. The Bible says that if any two of us will agree, we shall have whatever we are agreeing on. However, I must emphasize that what we are agreeing for must also be in agreement with the Word of God.

Matthew 18:19,20 (NAS)

"Again I say to you, that if two of you agree on earth about anything that they may ask, it shall be done for them by My Father who is in heaven. For where two or three have gathered together in My name, there I am in their midst."

V

KEEP YOUR HEALING

The problem I have found over the years is not people being healed, but people losing their healing. As I said in the second chapter of this book, many people are healed by my faith or someone else's faith, but often many of these people lose their healing. The reason for this is because Satan has stolen the Word that gave them their healing.

Mark 4:3-8,13-20 (NAS)

"Listen to this! Behold, the sower went out to sow; and it came about that as he was sowing, some seed fell beside the road, and the birds came and ate it up. And other seed fell on the rocky ground where it did not have much soil; and immediately it sprang up because it had no depth of soil. And after the sun had risen, it was scorched; and because it had no root, it withered away.

"And other seed fell among the thorns, and the thorns came up and choked it, and it yielded no crop. And other seeds fell into the

good soil and as they grew up and increased, they yielded a crop and produced thirty, sixty, and a hundredfold."

And He said to them, "Do you not understand this parable? And how will you understand all the parables? The sower sows the word. And these are the ones who are beside the road where the word is sown; and when they hear, immediately Satan comes and takes away [steals] *the word which has been sown in them.*

"And in a similar way these are the ones on whom seed was sown on the rocky places, who, when they hear the word, immediately receive it with joy; and they have no firm root in themselves, but are only temporary; then, when affliction or persecution arises because of the word, immediately they fall away.

"And others are the ones on whom seed was sown among the thorns; these are the ones who have heard the word, and the worries of the world, and the deceitfulness of riches, and the desires for other things enter in and choke the word, and it becomes unfruitful. And those are the ones on whom seed was sown on the good soil; and they hear the word and accept it, and bear fruit, thirty, sixty, and a hundredfold."

Many people hear the Word and it excites them. They grab the Word, but Satan quickly comes to steal it from them.

Be Careful What You Listen To

Mark 4:24 (AMP)

> *Be careful what you are hearing. The measure [of thought and study] you give [to the truth you hear] will be the measure [of virtue and knowledge] that comes back to you—and more [besides] will be given to you who hear.*

What you listen to before and after you are healed is very important. The devil will come to steal the Word from you if he can. He uses many different methods to do this. I have seen people healed. Then a friend comes up to them and says, "What are you doing without your crutches?" They say, "I was healed last night in the meeting at church." The friend replies, "You are crazy. Healing is not for today. You had better start using those crutches again." So they do, and they lose their healing. **We must not deny what God has done!**

I have seen deaf people healed. They could hear without their hearing aids, but after they returned to their seats, they put their hearing aids back on. When I asked them why they had done this, I would receive one of the following answers:

- One man said, "I just bought this new hearing aid. I do not want to waste my money." He lost his healing that night.
- One man's wife said, "He has been deaf for thirty years. He knows he cannot hear without his hearing aid." Even though two hundred people witnessed him hearing, he would not leave without wearing his hearing aid. He lost his healing also.
- I asked a woman who was healed in Canada why she put her hearing aid back on. She said, "I believe it is too good to be true."

God will not force healing on anyone. The choice is ours—we decide whether we want to receive and keep our healing or not.

The devil will use our friends to steal our healing from us, or he will use a lie to deceive us if we will listen to him. He will often use symptoms to deceive us. If we do not know the Word of God, and if we do not stand on the Word of God, he will steal our healing from us.

I have seen many people lose their healing because of a symptom the devil was trying to put on them. They did not know they had the right to stop him. They just accepted what he was offering to them.

Often someone will say, "They probably did not get healed in the first place." Let me tell you something! If I pray for someone who could not walk and they get up and walk, they were healed! If I pray for someone who could not hear and they can hear, they were healed! When I pray—or someone else prays—and the symptoms leave, that is healing. The healing may last for five minutes, five months, or for five years, but if your symptoms left, **you were healed!** Now the question is how do you keep your healing?

Four Things You Must Do To Keep Your Healing

1. First, you must recognize that Satan does not have the right to put sickness on you a second time.

Nahum 1:9

What do ye imagine against the Lord? he will make an utter end: ***affliction shall not rise up the second time.***

If Satan does not have the right to bring sickness back on us the second time, then what is this feeling? It is a lying symptom. The devil is trying to steal your healing. You say, "But it feels real." It must feel real or you would not accept it from him.

I have two testimonies of how Satan tried to steal the healings of two women I had prayed for.

The first lady was sixty-eight years old, and she had been deaf for nearly twenty years. After I prayed for her, she was able to hear even the least sound. In fact, the sound of birds singing woke her up the next morning. She told us that she had not been able to hear the birds chirping for many years. Her hearing was perfect for several days, and then one afternoon she noticed that she was having a difficult time understanding what her grandson was saying.

She came back to our evening service and asked me what she could do about her hearing problem. I shared Nahum 1:9 with her, which says that Satan cannot bring back an affliction the second time. She said, "What is happening to my ears, if he is not allowed to take my hearing away?" I told her that this was a lying symptom and that symptoms felt real. I reminded her that the devil was a liar and that he could not tell the truth. She got mad at the devil and began shouting at him, and her hearing cleared up immediately. Her son told me a few years later that his mother had lived until she was seventy-two years old, and she never had hearing problems again.

In 1990 I was in Austria, where I prayed for a woman who had several tumors in her breast. Because of these tumors, she had much pain and fear. I prayed for her and the tumors dissolved and the pain left her immediately.

Approximately three weeks later I received a telephone call from her, and she informed me that the pain had returned. I began to question her about the pain and found that the pain was not in the same place as it had been before, but that it was a similar pain. I reminded her of Nahum 1:9, explaining that Satan could not bring back an affliction the second time. I told her that this was a lying symptom and that she must do as James 4:7 says, and resist the devil. Then I had her speak to the devil and command him to take his lying symptom away. The pain left her immediately and she has had no reocurrence. Praise God!

2. Second, you must obey the Bible. You must **resist the devil**. When you do, **he will flee from you.**

James 4:7

Submit yourselves therefore to God. Resist the devil, and he will flee from you.

Notice that this scripture says you must resist the devil. It does not say if I resist the devil for you, he will flee from you. It says **if you resist the devil, he will flee from you**.

How can you resist the devil? You resist the devil the same way Jesus did. He is our Example.

Matthew 4:1-11 (NAS)

Then Jesus was led up by the Spirit into the wilderness to be tempted by the devil. And after He had fasted forty days and forty nights, He then became hungry. And the tempter came and said to Him, "If You are the Son of God, command that these stones become bread." But He answered and said, "It is written, 'MAN SHALL NOT LIVE ON BREAD ALONE, BUT ON EVERY WORD

THAT PROCEEDS OUT OF THE MOUTH OF GOD.'"

Then the devil took Him into the holy city; and he had Him stand on the pinnacle of the temple, and said to Him, "If You are the Son of God throw Yourself down; for it is written, 'HE WILL GIVE HIS ANGELS CHARGE CONCERNING YOU'; and 'ON THEIR HANDS THEY WILL BEAR YOU UP, LEST YOU STRIKE YOUR FOOT AGAINST A STONE.'" Jesus said to him, "On the other hand, it is written, 'YOU SHALL NOT PUT THE LORD YOUR GOD TO THE TEST.'"

Again, the devil took Him to a very high mountain, and showed Him all the kingdoms of the world, and their glory; and he said to Him, "All these things will I give You, if You fall down and worship me." Then Jesus said to him, "Begone, Satan! For it is written, 'YOU SHALL WORSHIP THE LORD YOUR GOD, AND SERVE HIM ONLY.'" ***Then the devil left Him.***

Notice that the key to Jesus resisting the devil was the Word of God. Every time the devil brings a temptation to you, throw God's Word at him, and he will flee from you.

Remember, when the devil tries to tempt you with sin, your weapon is, **"Devil, it is written, THOU SHALT NOT!"**

3. Realize that it is very important for YOU to keep the Word of God stirred up in your spirit. You keep the Word of God stirred up within you by regularly listening to healing scriptures or by regularly reading healing scriptures **out loud.**

If you are to use the Word of God as your weapon, you must know what God's Word says. It is very important to study God's Word. You must continually share what God has done for you, reminding yourself over and over, so that Satan cannot steal what God has given you.

I believe it is just as important to hear God's Word after you have been healed as it was before you were healed. Before you were healed, you were preparing to be healed as you listened to God's Word. After you are healed, God's Word will help you keep your healing. **His Word will strengthen you, help you, encourage you, and build you up,** giving you the ability to resist the devil. Praise God!

4. You must tell others what God has done for you.

When you tell others what God has done for you, you keep your faith stirred up. When you tell your children and grandchildren what God has done for you, you teach them to look to God when they have a need. This is why God told Israel to tell her children and grandchildren what He had done.

Deuteronomy 4:9 (NAS)

"Only give heed to yourself and keep your soul diligently, lest you forget the things which your eyes have seen, and lest they depart from your heart all the days of your life; but make them known to your sons and your grandsons."

In closing, I would like to leave this thought with you: If your sickness was caused by a physical habit such as smoking, drinking, or drugs, and God heals you, you should seek deliverance from the habit. If you are not delivered and you continue with this habit, the sickness may come back on you. Many times the sickness returns worse than it was in the beginning.

Likewise, if you have released bitterness or unforgiveness and received your healing, you should not allow yourself to go back and pick it up a second time. Those who go back and take up bitterness and unforgiveness will often have sickness return much worse than it was before they were healed.

Luke 11:24-26

When the unclean spirit is gone out of a man, he walketh through dry places, seeking rest; and finding none, he saith, I will return unto my house whence I came out. And when he cometh, he findeth it swept and garnished. Then goeth he, and taketh to him seven other spirits more wicked than himself; and they enter in, and dwell there: and the last state of that man is worse than the first.

These verses are talking about the deliverance of demons, but I believe this passage also teaches us a scriptural principle. When we have been healed or delivered from the hand of Satan, it is our responsibility to build up our spirit-man with God's Word so we will be able to resist Satan. Remember, the Word of God brings salvation, healing, and deliverance. When we fill our house with God's Word, then the house is full and Satan has no avenue of reentry.

VI

MAKE THESE SCRIPTURES A PART OF YOUR LIFE

Mark 4:24 (AMP)

Be careful what you are hearing. The measure [of thought and study] you give [to the truth you hear] will be the measure [of virtue and knowledge] that comes back to you—and more [besides] will be given to you who hear.

Hebrews 13:8 (NAS)

Jesus Christ is the same yesterday and today, yes and forever.

Acts 10:34 (NAS)

Peter said: "I most certainly understand how that God is not one to show partiality."

Isaiah 53:5 (NAS)

But He was pierced through for our transgressions, He was crushed for our iniquities;

the chastening for our well-being fell upon Him, and by His scourging [stripes] *we are healed.*

Psalm 103:1-5 (NAS)

Bless the Lord, O my soul; and all that is within me, bless His holy name. Bless the Lord, O my soul, and forget none of His benefits; who pardons all your iniquities; who heals all your diseases; who redeems your life from the pit; who crowns you with lovingkindness and compassion; who satisfies your years with good things, so that your youth is renewed like the eagle.

Proverbs 4:20-22 (NAS)

My son, give attention to my words; incline your ear to my sayings. Do not let them depart from your sight; keep them in the midst of your heart. For they are life to those who find them, and ***health to all their whole body.***

Psalm 107:19,20 (NAS)

Then they cried out to the Lord in their trouble; He saved them out of their distresses. He sent His Word and healed them, and delivered them from their destructions.

James 1:17 (NAS)

Every good thing bestowed and every perfect gift is from above, coming down from the

Father of lights, with whom there is no variation, or shifting shadow.

John 10:10 (NAS)

The thief [Satan] *comes only to steal, and kill, and destroy; I came that they might have life, and might have it abundantly.*

Jeremiah 30:17 (NAS)

"'For I will restore you to health and I will heal you of your wounds,' declares the Lord."

3 John 2

Beloved, I wish above all things that thou mayest prosper and be in health, even as thy soul prospereth.

Have You Accepted Christ?

If you have read this book and you are not sure that you have been born again, or if you have never **personally** asked Jesus to come into your life and forgive you of your sins, I invite you to pray the following prayer with me. According to Romans 10:9-13, you must personally ask God to forgive you of your sins. No one can do this for you.

Romans 10:9-13 (NAS)

If you confess with your mouth Jesus as Lord, and believe in your heart that God raised Him from the dead, you shall be saved; for with the heart man believes, resulting in righteousness, and with the mouth he confesses, resulting in salvation. For the Scripture says, "Whoever believes in Him will not be disappointed." For there is no distinction between Jew and Greek; for the same Lord is Lord of all, abounding in riches for all who call upon Him; for "Whoever will call upon the name of the Lord will be saved."

If you believe that Jesus died to pay the price for your sins and that God raised Him from the dead, **repeat this prayer with me:**

God, I am a sinner. Please forgive me of my sins. I accept Your Son, Jesus, as my

Savior, and I accept the price He paid for my sins (His blood).

Now, Father, I promise that I will read Your Word so I can find out what a Christian is like, and then I will act like a Christian. I will go to church on a regular basis—not just once or twice a year—so I can grow strong through the strength and encouragement of fellow Christians. I realize that we need each other. When I am weak, my church family will help and encourage me, and when others are weak, I will help and encourage them.

Father, because You have just forgiven me, I now forgive myself. I don't have the right to hold on to the things You have forgiven. Your Word says that my sins will never be remembered again. I thank You for this.

Father, I forgive those who have hurt me, and I ask that You also forgive them. I know they were deceived by Satan just as I was. Please send someone to tell them about Jesus so they too can become Christians. Thank You, Father. Amen.